BUILDING BLOCKS OF COMPUTER SCIENCE

ARTIFICIAL INTELLIGENCE

Written by Echo Elise González

Illustrated by Graham Ross

WORLD BOOK

www.worldbook.com

Co-published by agreement between Shi Tu Hui and World Book, Inc.

Shi Tu Hui
Room 1807, Block 1,
#3 West Dawang Road
Chaoyang District, Beijing 100025
P.R. China

World Book, Inc.
180 North LaSalle Street
Suite 900
Chicago, Illinois 60601
USA

© 2026. All rights reserved. This volume may not be reproduced in whole or in part in any form without prior written permission from the publisher.

WORLD BOOK and the GLOBE DEVICE are registered trademarks or trademarks of World Book, Inc.

Library of Congress Control Number: 2025938327
Building Blocks of Computer Science
ISBN: 978-0-7166-6706-3 (set, hard cover)

Artificial Intelligence
ISBN: 978-0-7166-6714-8 (hard cover)

Also available as:
ISBN: 978-0-7166-6724-7 (soft cover)
ISBN: 978-0-7166-6734-6 (e-book)

WORLD BOOK STAFF

Editorial

Vice President
Tom Evans

Senior Manager, New Content
Jeff De La Rosa

Manager, New Product Development
Nicholas Kilzer

Associate Manager, New Content
William D. Adams

Content Creator
Elizabeth Huyck

Proofreader
Nathalie Strassheim

Graphics and Design

Senior Visual Communications Designer
Melanie Bender

Acknowledgments
Writer: Echo Elise González
Illustrator: Graham Ross/The Bright Agency
Series reviewed by George K. Thiruvathukal (Loyola University Chicago); Peter Jang (Actualize Coding Bootcamp)

TABLE OF CONTENTS

What Is Artificial Intelligence? 4
How Is AI Different? 8
Machine Learning 10
AI in Training 14
Supervised Learning 16
Unsupervised Learning 18
Machine Brains 20
Can AI Get Creative? 26
The Future of Artificial Intelligence 28
Using AI Responsibly 30
Timeline 32
Activity: How Would You Draw for AI? 34
Can You Believe It?! 36
Words to Know 39
Index 40

There is a glossary on page 39. Terms defined in the glossary are in type **that looks like this** on their first appearance.

"What do you feel like listening to?"

"You may already have met an AI program. They power search engines..."

"If you liked that song, try this one!"

"Recommend films and music you might like..."

"How can I assist you today?"

"Write me a poem that rhymes!"

"A robot tried to make a pie
But confused the sugar for the sky.
So it made a tart that could fly."

"And chat in online **chatbots**."

5

AI can also learn to play games. In 1997, an early AI called Deep Blue beat a world chess champion at a game of chess.

SmartBot, what's the most unusual animal on every continent?

Some of the most endangered animals on each continent are:
North America: red wolf
South America: glass frog
Eurasia: ...

AI is good at many things..

Tell me a joke with a pun.

What did one wheel say to the other?

You look tired!

Ha Ha Ha

Some AI **models** can sound friendly, like a real person.

HOW IS AI DIFFERENT?

How is AI able to accomplish such amazing feats?

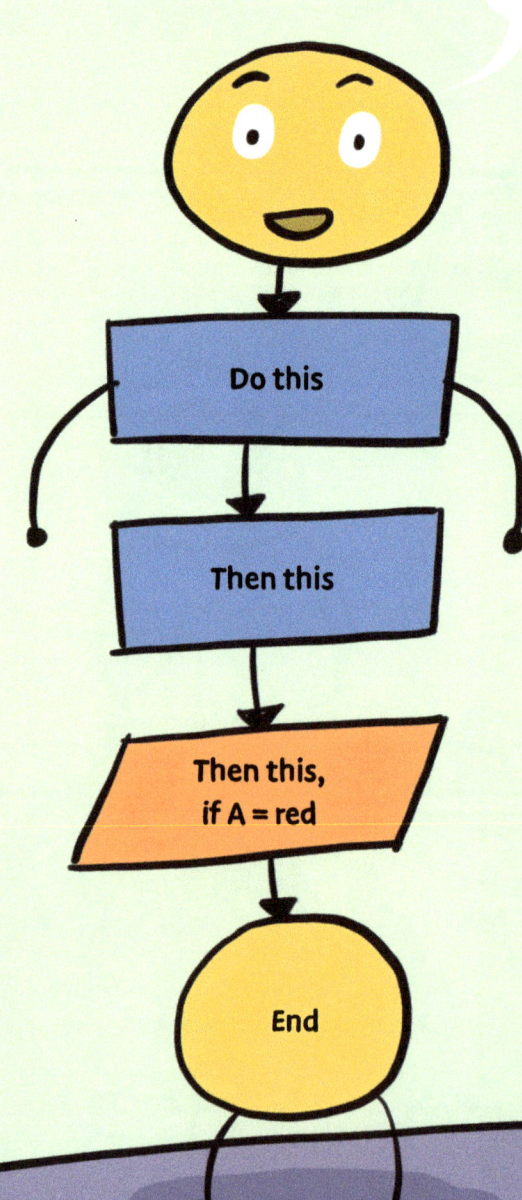

Hi, I'm Algorithm!

Ordinary computer **algorithms** break down tasks into a series of steps for the computer to follow.

These instructions may tell the computer to do different things based on input.

But the computer can't do anything that hasn't been programmed in.

Panel 1:

SmartBot is a robot with AI. SmartBot can change what it does based on information it collects.

SmartBot, give each plant as much water as it needs to stay green.

5 cups

I gave this one more water but now it is yellow. Try less water next week.

3 cups

1 cup

Panel 2:

AI models can improve their performance with more data, kind of like how people learn from experience. This is called machine learning.

In future, cilantro will get less water.

13

Fast   Far   Stunt

What do paper airplanes have in common?

What folds make which shape?

Which fly the best?

The AI program looks for patterns in the training set, like the sequence of folds to make each plane.

To test how well the AI has learned, I use some examples that it has not seen before. This is called the **verification set**.

SmartBot, which of these two planes you've never seen before will fly better?

Based on my analysis of 12,400 designs, this one has a 70% chance of flying better.

15

MACHINE BRAINS

You have a brain to think with. AI uses a computer.

Or lots of them! The most powerful AI programs run on banks of big computers. Your phone or computer connects to these when you use an AI.

All those computers use a LOT of electricity!

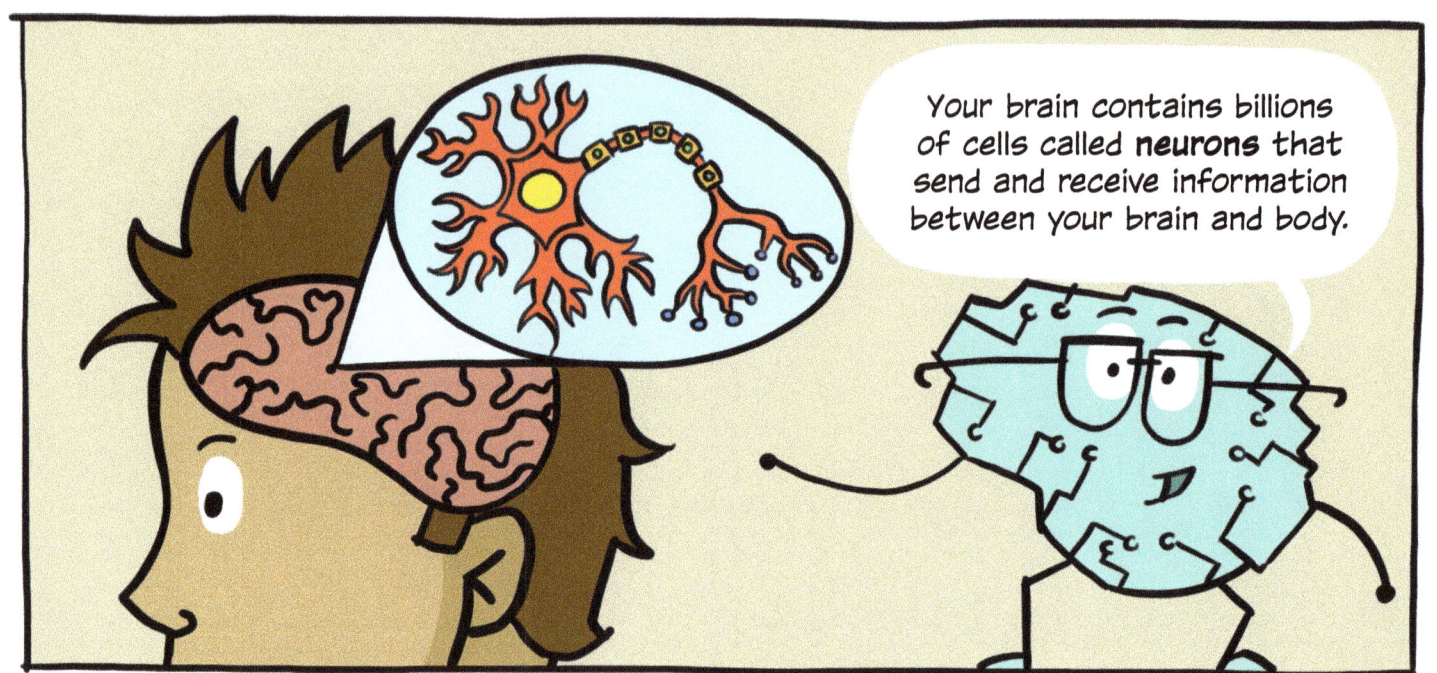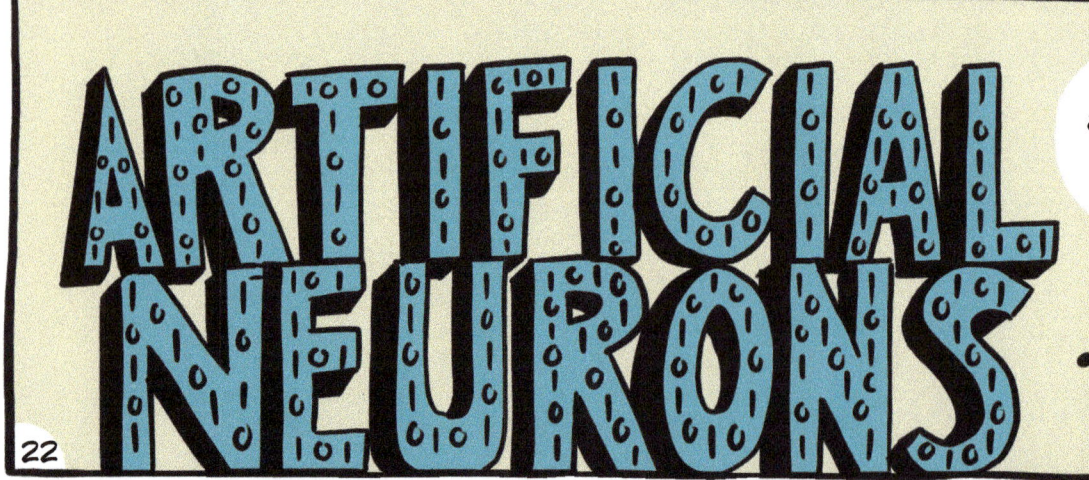

CAN AI GET CREATIVE?

Advanced AI programs can draw pictures, have conversations, and invent recipes.

They do this by breaking down pictures or sentences into patterns, then making new examples to fit the same pattern.

I have shown SmartBot many paintings of trees.

SmartBot, paint me a picture of a tree that is not exactly like any you have seen.

Computing pixel pattern for tree different by 10%

Art created!

AI can combine patterns in new ways. But even advanced AI can't tell if its pictures are any good. That still requires human intelligence.

While human beings are capable of original and creative thought...

AI is only able to produce creative output based on its programming and examples it has seen.

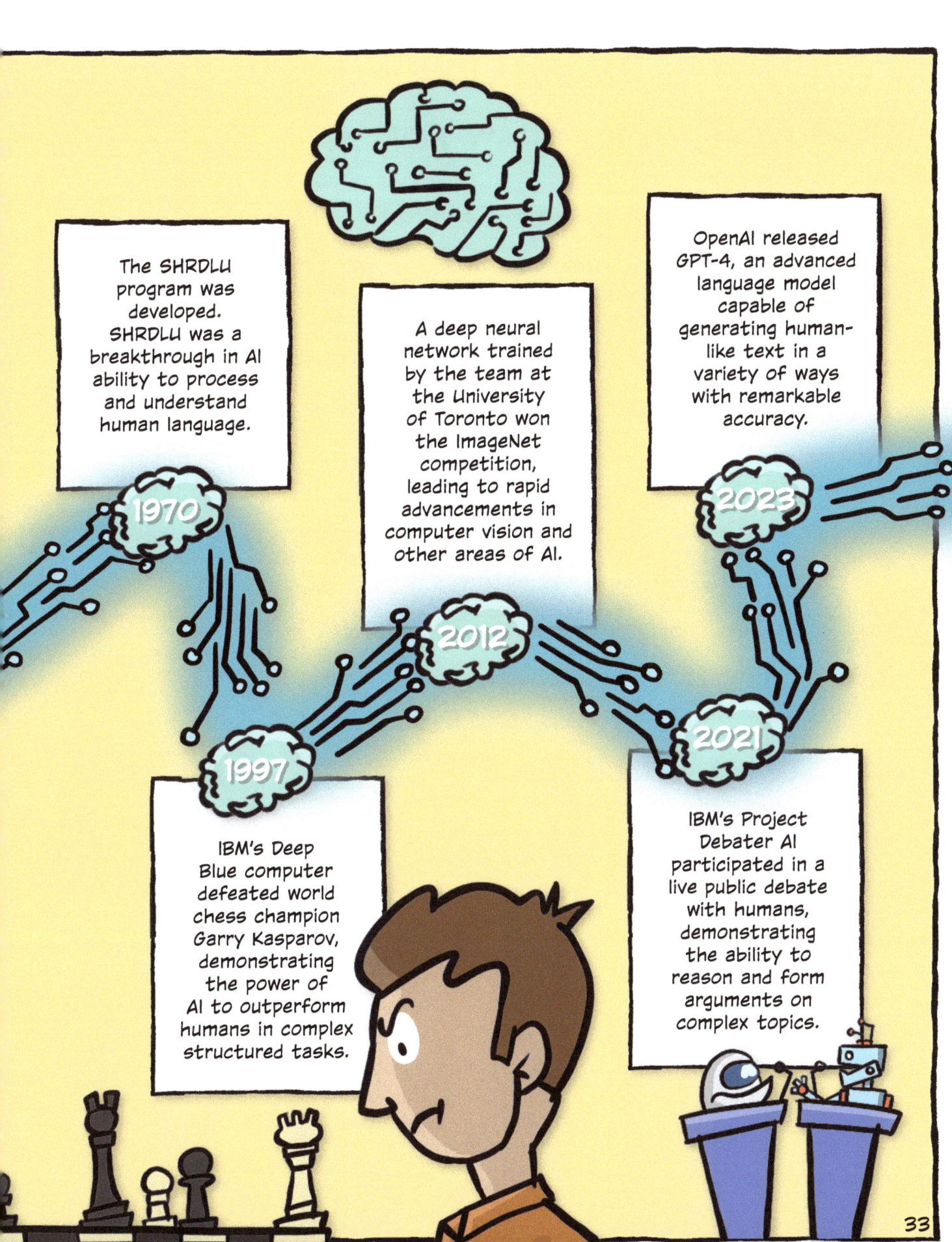

ACTIVITY:
HOW WOULD YOU DRAW FOR AI?

AI programs can "learn" how humans express themselves by studying thousands and even millions of examples. These examples are often images—including photographs, paintings, and drawings—of faces that convey emotions. But what features does an AI program focus on to learn different human emotions or expressions?

Here's a little exercise that will help you understand what features AI might focus on and use to understand human thoughts and feelings. All you need is some paper and a pencil. Your task is to draw faces that could be used to train an AI to recognize such expressions as happiness, sadness, surprise, or anger.

Write or draw some human emotions on a piece of paper. For example, draw a happy face. Now, what features of your drawing tell you that the person whose face you drew is happy?

Create a table of information to look for patterns in the data.

What tells us that a person is happy, sad, or angry?

Emotion	Features
Happy	• Smiling • Raised eyebrows • Eyes wide open • Puffy cheeks • Teeth showing • Lips facing up
Sad	• • •
Angry	• • •

Now try with these emotions and feelings: **surprised; afraid; excited; sleepy; nervous; bored;** and **annoyed**. Maybe you can think of more feelings to express and draw.

These drawings will help an AI understand how to "see" and interpret emotions, much like how we do!

Let your imagination run wild as you draw, and think about how these simple images can tell a story about feelings! Can you think of other emotions or feelings you can describe with just a face?

Compare your descriptions of features with others. How do your descriptions compare? What features are used to convey each emotion?

CAN YOU BELIEVE IT?!

American author Isaac Asimov's novel *I, Robot* (1950) helped popularize the concept of

intelligent machines

long before they became a reality.

The lack of funding and progress on AI during the 1970's and 1980's is referred to as the

"AI Winter"

by computer experts. AI research saw a major resurgence in the late 1990's, driven by better algorithms and computing power.

The first AI program, created in the 1950's, was a

checkers-playing program.

It could evaluate possible moves and make decisions based on them.

AI has been a key component of

space exploration.

AI helps spacecraft make real-time decisions without waiting for instructions from Earth, crucial for long-distance missions.

AI programs can generate

original music

in various genres, from classical to jazz, often indistinguishable from compositions made by human artists.

In 2011, the IBM computer Watson competed and won on a

TV quiz show.

Watson's ability to understand natural language and process vast amounts of information in real time made Watson a champion.

In 2016, an AI program named *AlphaGo* defeated a human world champion at the

board game Go,

a game that's much more complicated than chess!

In 2021, an

AI-created painting

was sold for over

$432,000

at an auction!

AI is now used to

help doctors detect diseases

in X rays and other medical images, sometimes with even better accuracy than human doctors!

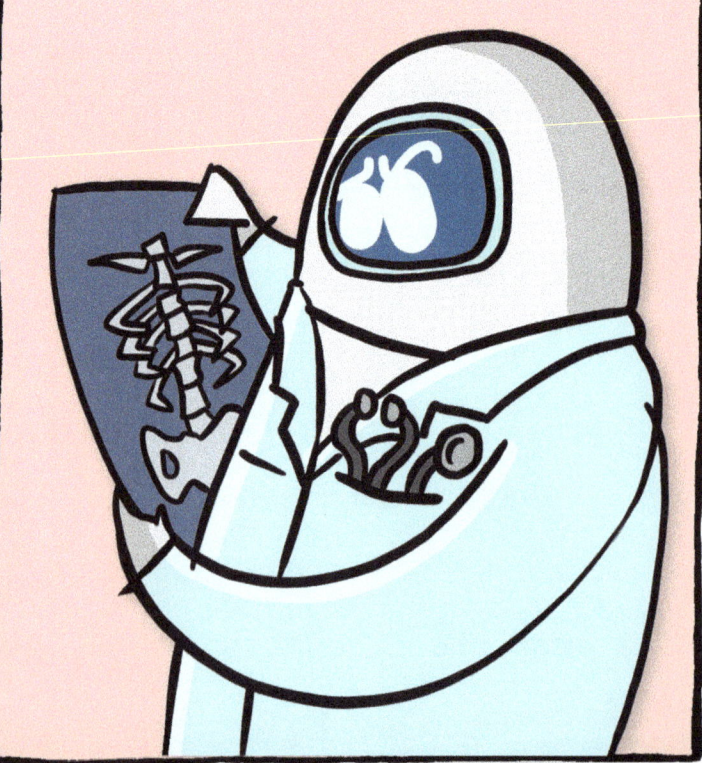

WORDS TO KNOW

AI model an artificial intelligence program that has been designed to do a specific task.

algorithm a set of step-by-step instructions used to write computer programs. Algorithms are also used to solve math and other problems.

artificial intelligence (AI) a kind of computer program that uses data and logic to solve complex problems.

artificial neural network (ANN) a computer program that mimics the way human brains process information.

chatbot an AI model (program) designed to chat or answer questions in a humanlike way. Chatbots analyze lots of written text and predict what words are most likely to come next, moment to moment.

consciousness having self-awareness and the capacity to think, feel, and imagine.

data information that a computer processes or stores.

general intelligence the ability to master different skills and learn any new thing.

input information coming in to a computer program.

logic rules for making correct decisions and deductions.

neuron a nerve cell.

output information flowing out of a computer program (such as the answer to a problem).

program a series of instructions for a computer to follow.

supervised learning training an AI model by giving it pre-labeled data sets.

training set a collection of data that is used to teach, or train, an AI model.

unsupervised learning letting an AI model figure out the best way to solve problems by trial and error.

verification set a collection of new data used to test an AI model.

INDEX

algorithms, 8-9, 12
artificial intelligence (AI), 4-9 creativity
  of, 26-27, 31
  errors in, 27, 30
  future of, 28-29
  models, 6, 9, 13, 14, 23, 29, 30
  programs, 4-5, 7-16, 19-21, 26, 29, 31
  responsible use of, 30-31
  risks of, 29-31
artificial neural network (ANN), 21-23
artificial neurons, 22-23

brain, human, 20-22

chatbots, 5
computer programmers, 10, 16
computer programs, 4-5, 8-12, 31. See also artificial intelligence programs
consciousness, 7

data, 9, 12-14, 17, 24
Deep Blue, 7

general intelligence, 14

input, 8, 17
input layers, 24

logic, 9

machine learning, 10-13

neurons, 22

output, 26
output layers, 25

Perceptron, 21

Rosenblatt, Frank, 21

supervised learning, 16-17, 19

training sets, 14-15

unsupervised learning, 18-19

verification sets, 15

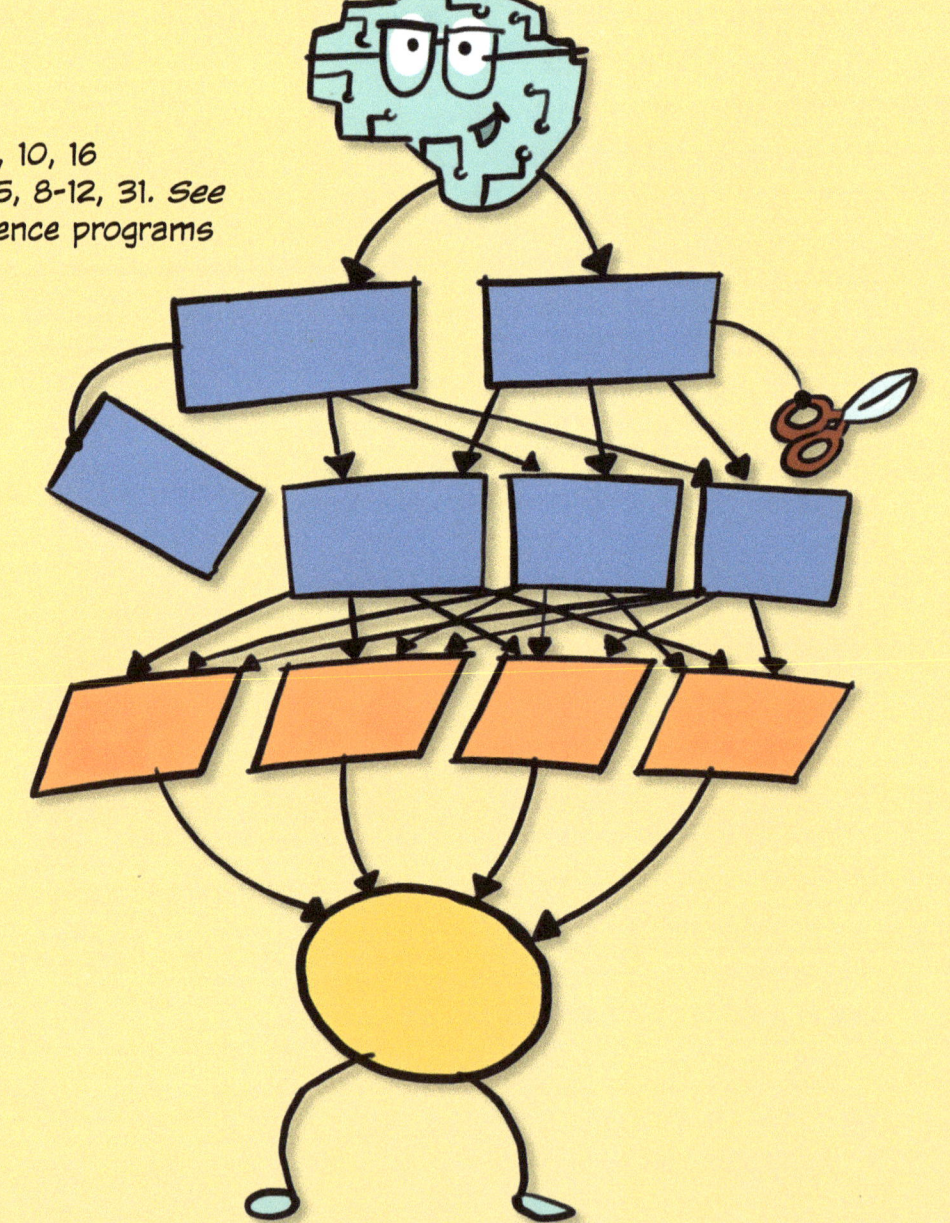

www.ingramcontent.com/pod-product-compliance
Lightning Source LLC
Chambersburg PA
CBHW061256170426
43191CB00041B/2432